The Real Estate Financial Planner

Budgeting, Funding and Investing

NELLA BYRAN

Copyright

No part of this should be reproduced without the permission of the author.

© Nella Byran 2024

Contents

Introduction	4
Understanding Real Estate as an Investment	8
The Basics of Real Estate Investment	9
Why Real Estate?	11
Setting Financial Goals for Real Estate Investment	15
Short-term vs Long-term Goals	15
Aligning Goals with Investment Strategies	17
Creating a Real Estate Investment Budget	20
Assessing Your Current Financial Situation	20
Estimating Costs and Revenues	21
Managing Personal Finances	24
Building a Strong Financial Foundation	24
Debt Management and Savings Strategies	26
Evaluating Potential Properties	29
Research and Analysis Techniques	29
Determining Property Value	32
Exploring Funding Options	35
Traditional Mortgages	35
Alternative Financing Methods	37
Securing Financing	42
Preparing for Loan Applications	42
Understanding Loan Terms and Conditions	45
Creative Financing Strategies	49
Owner Financing	49
Partnering and Syndication	52
Leveraging Equity	57

- Home Equity Loans and Lines of Credit 57
- Using Equity in Other Properties 59
- Real Estate Investment Strategies 63
  - Buy and Hold Investments 63
  - Property Flipping...66
- Investing in Rental Properties 70
  - Selecting Profitable Rental Properties....................................70
  - Managing Tenants and Rental Income 73
- Commercial Real Estate Investments..78
  - Types of Commercial Properties...78
  - Evaluating Commercial Investment Opportunities 82
- Real Estate Investment Trusts (REITs) 87
  - Understanding REITs 87
  - Benefits of Investing in REITs...90
  - Risks of Investing in REITs 92
- Property Management Best Practices...95
  - Maintenance and Repairs 95
  - Hiring Professional Property Managers 99
- Tax Planning and Real Estate...104
  - Understanding Real Estate Taxes...104
  - Tax Benefits and Deductions..107
- Building and Diversifying Your Portfolio................................112
  - Long-term Growth Strategies...112
  - Diversifying Across Property Types and Locations..........115
- Conclusion: Reflecting on Your Real Estate Journey 119
  - Adapting to Market Changes and Trends..........................121

Introduction

Real estate investment stands as a cornerstone of wealth creation and financial stability for countless individuals and families worldwide. Whether you're a seasoned investor or just beginning to explore the potential of real estate, understanding the fundamentals of budgeting, securing funding, and making strategic investments is crucial. "The Real Estate Financial Planner: Budgeting, Funding, and Investing" serves as your comprehensive guide through this multifaceted landscape, offering practical insights and expert advice to help you navigate the complexities and capitalize on the opportunities available in real estate.

At its core, this book is designed to empower you with the knowledge and tools necessary to make informed decisions at every stage of your real estate investment journey. From setting clear financial goals to evaluating properties, from exploring diverse funding options to implementing effective investment strategies, each chapter is crafted to provide clarity and direction. Whether your objective is to build a diverse portfolio of rental properties, embark on the rewarding path of property flipping, or explore the potential of commercial real estate, this book equips you with the essential skills to succeed.

Understanding the financial implications of real estate investments is pivotal. Hence, we delve into the intricacies of budgeting, ensuring you have a solid foundation in financial planning tailored specifically for real estate ventures. Furthermore, we explore various funding avenues—from traditional mortgages to innovative financing methods—guiding you on how to secure the capital needed to turn your investment dreams into reality.

Moreover, "The Real Estate Financial Planner" emphasizes the importance of strategic decision-making in maximizing returns and managing risks. Whether you're managing properties yourself or employing professional property managers, effective property management is crucial to preserving asset value and enhancing profitability. Additionally, the book addresses the tax implications of real estate investments, offering insights into how to leverage tax benefits and deductions to optimize your financial outcomes.

Throughout these pages, we emphasize the value of adaptability and foresight in an ever-evolving real estate market. By understanding market trends and economic indicators, you'll be better equipped to make informed decisions that align with your investment goals. Ultimately, our goal is to empower you to build a sustainable and profitable real estate portfolio that supports your long-term financial objectives.

"The Real Estate Financial Planner: Budgeting, Funding, and Investing" is more than just a guide—it's a roadmap to financial independence through real estate. Whether you're aiming to diversify your investments, generate passive income, or secure your financial future, this book provides the knowledge and strategies to help you achieve your aspirations in the dynamic world of real estate investment.

Understanding Real Estate as an Investment

Real estate investment represents a fundamental pillar of wealth accumulation and financial security for individuals and institutions alike. At its core, real estate investment involves the acquisition, ownership, management, rental, or sale of real estate for profit. Unlike stocks or bonds, which are intangible assets, real estate offers tangible benefits such as physical land, buildings, and improvements. This tangible nature provides investors with a sense of security and a visible asset that can appreciate in value over time.

Investing in real estate spans a spectrum of opportunities, from residential properties such as single-family homes and condominiums to commercial properties like office buildings, retail centers, and industrial complexes. Each type of property presents unique advantages and challenges, catering to different investment strategies and financial goals. Understanding these nuances is essential for investors to make informed decisions and capitalize on the potential returns offered by real estate.

The Basics of Real Estate Investment

Successful real estate investment begins with a solid understanding of its fundamental principles. Key considerations include property valuation, cash flow analysis, financing options, market trends, and risk management. Property valuation involves assessing the current market value of a property based on factors such as location, condition, comparable sales, and income potential for rental properties.

Cash flow analysis is crucial for evaluating the financial performance of an investment property. It involves calculating the potential rental income minus expenses such as mortgage payments, property taxes, insurance, maintenance costs, and vacancies. Positive cash flow indicates that the property generates more income than expenses, while negative cash flow may require additional financial planning or adjustments in investment strategy.

Financing options play a pivotal role in real estate investment, as most investors leverage borrowed capital to acquire properties. Traditional financing methods include mortgages offered by banks and financial institutions, which typically require a down payment and adherence to strict lending criteria. Alternative financing options, such as seller financing, private loans, or partnerships, provide flexibility for investors who may not qualify for traditional loans or seek creative funding solutions.

Market trends and economic indicators influence real estate investment decisions, as fluctuations in supply and demand, interest rates, employment rates, and demographic shifts impact property values and rental income potential. Staying informed about market conditions and conducting thorough market research enables investors to identify emerging opportunities and mitigate risks associated with market volatility.

Risk management is essential in real estate investment, encompassing strategies to minimize potential risks such as property depreciation, tenant turnover, legal liabilities, and unexpected expenses. Diversification across different types of properties, geographic locations, and investment strategies can reduce overall portfolio risk and enhance long-term investment performance.

Why Real Estate?

Real estate investment offers several compelling advantages that distinguish it from other investment vehicles. One of the primary benefits is the potential for appreciation in property value over time. Historically, real estate has shown resilience and the ability to increase in value, providing investors with the opportunity to build equity and wealth through capital gains.

Income generation is another attractive feature of real estate investment, particularly through rental properties. Rental income can provide investors with a steady stream of passive income, which can supplement other sources of revenue or serve as a primary source of financial stability during retirement.

Moreover, real estate investment offers tax advantages that can significantly enhance overall investment returns. Deductions such as mortgage interest, property taxes, depreciation expenses, and operating expenses can reduce taxable income generated from rental properties, thereby lowering tax liabilities and increasing cash flow for investors.

Additionally, real estate investment provides investors with a tangible asset that offers intrinsic value and utility. Unlike stocks or bonds, which can fluctuate in value based on market sentiment or economic conditions, real estate provides stability and a physical presence that can be utilized for residential, commercial, or industrial purposes.

Furthermore, real estate investment allows for portfolio diversification, reducing overall investment risk by spreading capital across different asset classes. Diversification enables investors to balance potential returns with varying levels of risk, ensuring a resilient investment strategy that can withstand market volatility and economic uncertainties.

Real estate investment represents a dynamic and multifaceted opportunity for investors seeking to build wealth, generate income, and achieve long-term financial security. By understanding the fundamentals of real estate as an investment, including property valuation, cash flow analysis, financing options, market trends, and risk management strategies, investors can make informed decisions that align with their financial goals and capitalize on the unique advantages offered by real estate.

Setting Financial Goals for Real Estate Investment

Setting clear and achievable financial goals is paramount to success in real estate investment. Whether you're aiming to generate passive income, build equity, achieve financial independence, or diversify your investment portfolio, defining specific goals provides a roadmap for decision-making and strategy development. Financial goals in real estate investment should be SMART—Specific, Measurable, Achievable, Relevant, and Time-bound—to ensure clarity and accountability throughout the investment process.

Short-term vs Long-term Goals

In real estate investment, distinguishing between short-term and long-term goals is essential for establishing a balanced and sustainable investment strategy. Short-term goals typically focus on immediate objectives such as acquiring a property, completing renovations, and generating initial rental income or resale profit within a few months to a few years. These goals are geared towards achieving quick returns on investment and capitalizing on market opportunities in the short term.

On the other hand, long-term goals encompass broader objectives that extend over an extended period, ranging from five to ten years or more. Long-term goals in real estate investment may include building a diversified portfolio of income-producing properties, leveraging equity for future acquisitions, and creating a stable and reliable source of passive income for retirement or wealth preservation. These goals require strategic planning, patience, and a commitment to enduring market fluctuations and economic cycles.

Balancing short-term and long-term goals is crucial for maintaining financial stability and mitigating risks associated with real estate investment. Short-term goals provide immediate gratification and liquidity, while long-term goals offer sustained growth and stability through asset appreciation, income generation, and portfolio diversification.

Aligning Goals with Investment Strategies

Aligning financial goals with investment strategies is instrumental in maximizing the efficiency and effectiveness of real estate investment initiatives. Each investment strategy—such as buy and hold, property flipping, rental properties, commercial real estate, or real estate investment trusts (REITs)—serves distinct purposes and requires a tailored approach to goal achievement.

For instance, investors pursuing buy-and-hold strategies typically aim to accumulate properties with long-term appreciation potential and stable rental income. Aligning goals with this strategy involves identifying properties in high-demand locations, conducting thorough due diligence, securing competitive financing, and implementing proactive property management practices to optimize cash flow and property value over time.

Conversely, investors engaged in property flipping strategies prioritize short-term gains by purchasing distressed properties, renovating or upgrading them, and selling them at a profit within a relatively brief timeframe. Aligning goals with this strategy necessitates meticulous market analysis, budgeting for renovation costs, understanding local market trends, and executing timely sales to capitalize on market demand and maximize return on investment (ROI).

Moreover, aligning financial goals with investment strategies requires continuous evaluation and adaptation to evolving market conditions, economic factors, and investor objectives. Regularly reassessing goals, refining strategies, and leveraging professional expertise—including real estate agents, financial advisors, and legal counsel—enhances the likelihood of achieving desired outcomes and mitigating potential risks associated with real estate investment.

Setting clear and achievable financial goals, distinguishing between short-term and long-term objectives, and aligning goals with appropriate investment strategies are critical components of successful real estate investment. By embracing a structured approach to goal setting and strategy development, investors can navigate the complexities of the real estate market, capitalize on opportunities, and achieve sustainable financial growth and prosperity over time.

Creating a Real Estate Investment Budget

A well-structured budget is essential for successful real estate investment, providing a framework to manage expenses, allocate resources effectively, and achieve financial goals. Creating a real estate investment budget begins with a thorough assessment of your financial capabilities, followed by a detailed analysis of projected costs and anticipated revenues. This process ensures that you can make informed decisions, maintain financial discipline, and maximize the profitability of your investment endeavors.

Assessing Your Current Financial Situation

Before diving into real estate investment, it's crucial to conduct a comprehensive assessment of your current financial situation. This evaluation includes reviewing your income sources, savings, investments, debts, credit score, and overall financial stability. Understanding your financial standing provides clarity on how much capital you can allocate towards real estate investment, the level of risk you can comfortably undertake, and your ability to secure financing if necessary.

Assessing your current financial situation also involves evaluating your liquidity, or access to cash and credit, which is essential for covering initial investment costs, property acquisition expenses, and ongoing operational expenses such as maintenance, property management fees, and unforeseen repairs. Additionally, reviewing your debt-to-income ratio and creditworthiness helps determine your eligibility for mortgage loans and other financing options, ensuring that you can leverage external capital to expand your investment portfolio strategically.

Estimating Costs and Revenues

Estimating costs and revenues is a critical component of creating a realistic and sustainable real estate investment budget. Costs associated with real estate investment encompass various expenses, including property acquisition costs (e.g., purchase price, closing costs, appraisal fees), renovation and repair expenses (e.g., remodeling, repairs, upgrades), financing costs (e.g., loan origination fees, interest payments), property taxes, insurance premiums, and ongoing maintenance and operational costs.

To accurately estimate costs, conducting thorough market research and due diligence is essential. This involves evaluating comparable property sales, analyzing local market trends, and assessing potential rental income or resale values. Projecting revenues entails forecasting rental income based on market rental rates, vacancy rates, tenant turnover, and potential appreciation in property value over time. Realistic revenue projections help gauge the profitability and return on investment (ROI) potential of a property, guiding investment decisions and budget allocations accordingly.

Furthermore, incorporating contingency reserves into your budget is prudent to account for unexpected expenses, economic downturns, or unforeseen repairs that may arise during property ownership. Maintaining a conservative approach to budgeting ensures financial resilience and minimizes the risk of budget overruns, enabling you to navigate fluctuations in the real estate market and sustain long-term investment success.

Creating a real estate investment budget involves assessing your current financial situation, estimating costs and revenues accurately, and incorporating contingency planning to optimize financial outcomes and mitigate risks. By adopting a disciplined and strategic approach to budgeting, investors can maximize profitability, achieve financial goals, and build a robust portfolio of real estate assets that generates sustainable income and long-term wealth accumulation.

Managing Personal Finances

Effective management of personal finances forms the cornerstone of successful real estate investment. It involves adopting disciplined financial practices, setting clear financial goals, and establishing a solid foundation to support your investment endeavors. Managing personal finances encompasses various aspects, including budgeting, saving, debt management, and enhancing financial literacy to make informed decisions that align with your long-term financial objectives.

Building a Strong Financial Foundation

Building a strong financial foundation is essential before venturing into real estate investment. This foundation begins with creating and adhering to a comprehensive budget that tracks income sources and expenses, allowing you to allocate funds towards savings, investments, and debt repayment effectively. Establishing an emergency fund provides a financial safety net to cover unexpected expenses or income disruptions, ensuring stability and mitigating the need to liquidate real estate assets prematurely.

Moreover, building a strong credit profile through responsible borrowing and timely debt repayment enhances your ability to secure favorable financing options for real estate investment. This includes maintaining a favorable debt-to-income ratio, managing credit card balances, and monitoring your credit score to qualify for competitive mortgage rates and terms.

Investing in financial education and seeking guidance from financial advisors or wealth management professionals can also strengthen your financial foundation. Understanding investment strategies, risk management techniques, and tax implications empowers you to make informed decisions and optimize returns on real estate investments while mitigating potential risks.

Debt Management and Savings Strategies

Effectively managing debt and implementing savings strategies are integral components of sound financial planning for real estate investment. Debt management involves prioritizing high-interest debt repayment, such as credit cards or personal loans, to reduce financial liabilities and improve cash flow for investment opportunities. Consolidating debts through refinancing or debt consolidation loans can lower interest rates and streamline repayment schedules, freeing up funds for savings and investment purposes.

Savings strategies focus on systematically setting aside funds for future real estate investments, retirement planning, and achieving financial milestones. Establishing automatic transfers to designated savings accounts or investment vehicles, such as individual retirement accounts (IRAs) or employer-sponsored retirement plans, facilitates disciplined savings habits and capitalizes on compound interest over time.

Furthermore, diversifying savings across liquid and low-risk investments, such as money market accounts or certificates of deposit (CDs), balances liquidity with capital preservation while maintaining accessibility for short-term financial goals or emergency needs. As savings accumulate, strategically allocating funds towards real estate investments aligned with your risk tolerance, investment horizon, and financial objectives maximizes portfolio growth and wealth accumulation.

In conclusion, managing personal finances, building a strong financial foundation, and implementing effective debt management and savings strategies are essential prerequisites for successful real estate investment. By prioritizing financial discipline, cultivating savings habits, and optimizing debt utilization, investors can enhance their financial well-being, capitalize on investment opportunities, and achieve long-term financial prosperity through real estate.

Evaluating Potential Properties

Evaluating potential properties is a critical step in the real estate investment process, requiring thorough research, meticulous analysis, and informed decision-making to identify properties that align with your investment goals and financial objectives. This comprehensive evaluation encompasses various aspects, including market research, financial analysis, property inspections, and assessing potential risks and rewards associated with property ownership.

Research and Analysis Techniques

Conducting extensive research is essential to gather relevant information and data points that inform your property evaluation process. Research techniques include studying local real estate market trends, analyzing comparable property sales (comps), assessing neighborhood demographics and amenities, and evaluating economic indicators impacting property values and rental demand.

Market research involves identifying emerging or established neighborhoods with potential for appreciation and rental income growth. Analyzing historical property data, vacancy rates, and rental yield metrics provides insights into market dynamics and investment opportunities. Additionally, exploring local zoning laws, property tax rates, and regulatory changes ensures compliance and mitigates legal risks associated with property ownership.

Financial analysis techniques involve calculating key performance indicators (KPIs) such as return on investment (ROI), cash-on-cash return, and cap rate (capitalization rate) to assess the profitability and financial viability of potential properties. Evaluating income potential through rental income projections, expense forecasts, and vacancy rates helps gauge cash flow stability and long-term investment returns.

Property inspections and due diligence play a crucial role in assessing the physical condition and structural integrity of potential properties. Conducting professional inspections, reviewing maintenance records, and identifying potential renovation or repair costs enables investors to estimate property improvement expenses accurately and negotiate purchase terms based on property condition.

Risk assessment involves identifying and mitigating potential risks associated with property investments, such as environmental hazards, property title issues, insurance coverage, and market volatility. Implementing risk management strategies, such as diversifying investment portfolios, securing adequate insurance coverage, and conducting comprehensive property appraisals, safeguards against unforeseen challenges and protects investment capital.

Determining Property Value

Determining property value is a fundamental aspect of evaluating potential properties and making informed investment decisions. Property valuation methods encompass both quantitative and qualitative approaches to assess market value, intrinsic worth, and investment potential.

Quantitative valuation methods utilize comparative market analysis (CMA) to evaluate recent property sales data and comparable properties (comps) in the same neighborhood or market area. Analyzing sold prices, square footage, property condition, and amenities helps establish a fair market value (FMV) and competitive pricing strategy for potential acquisitions.

Appraisal methods involve hiring certified real estate appraisers to conduct professional property valuations based on industry standards, legal guidelines, and property-specific characteristics. Appraisers assess property condition, location, comparable sales, and income potential to generate unbiased appraisals that lenders and investors use to determine loan eligibility and investment feasibility.

Qualitative valuation considerations include assessing intangible factors such as property aesthetics, neighborhood desirability, proximity to schools, parks, and public amenities, and future development potential. Evaluating qualitative aspects enhances investment decision-making by incorporating subjective factors that influence property value perception and market demand among potential buyers or renters.

Evaluating potential properties involves employing research and analysis techniques, conducting thorough due diligence, and determining property value through quantitative and qualitative valuation methods. By integrating comprehensive evaluation strategies into the investment process, investors can identify lucrative opportunities, mitigate risks, and maximize returns on real estate investments aligned with their financial goals and investment objectives.

Exploring Funding Options

Exploring funding options is a crucial aspect of real estate investment, as it determines how investors can finance property acquisitions and leverage capital to maximize investment potential. Understanding different funding options, including traditional mortgages and alternative financing methods, enables investors to tailor their financial strategies to align with their investment goals and risk tolerance.

Traditional Mortgages

Traditional mortgages represent one of the most common and accessible forms of financing for real estate investment. Offered by banks, credit unions, and mortgage lenders, traditional mortgages typically require a down payment ranging from 3% to 20% of the property's purchase price, depending on the lender's requirements and loan program. Key features of traditional mortgages include:

- **Fixed-Rate Mortgages:** These mortgages offer stable monthly payments and interest rates over the loan term, usually 15 to 30 years. Fixed-rate mortgages provide predictability and protection against interest rate fluctuations, making them suitable for investors seeking long-term property ownership and stable cash flow from rental income.

- **Adjustable-Rate Mortgages (ARMs):** ARMs feature initial fixed-rate periods followed by adjustable interest rates based on market indexes. While ARMs offer lower initial interest rates and monthly payments, they entail potential payment adjustments and increased financial risks associated with interest rate fluctuations.

- **Government-Backed Loans:** Programs such as FHA (Federal Housing Administration) loans and VA (Veterans

Affairs) loans provide favorable terms and lower down payment requirements for eligible borrowers, making homeownership more accessible for first-time buyers and veterans. These loans often include mortgage insurance premiums (MIP) or funding fees to protect lenders against default risks.

- ❖ **Conventional Loans:** Conventional mortgages are not insured or guaranteed by government entities, offering flexible loan terms, competitive interest rates, and options for both primary residences and investment properties. Conventional loans typically require higher credit scores and down payments compared to government-backed loans but provide greater flexibility and financing options for real estate investors.

Alternative Financing Methods

In addition to traditional mortgages, real estate investors can explore alternative financing methods to acquire properties and optimize capital utilization. Alternative financing options cater to investors who may not qualify for conventional loans or seek innovative funding solutions tailored to specific investment strategies. Key alternative financing methods include:

❖ **Private Lenders and Hard Money Loans:** Private lenders, individuals, or private investment firms offer hard money loans based on property value rather than borrower creditworthiness. Hard money loans feature shorter loan terms, higher interest rates, and lower loan-to-value (LTV) ratios, making them suitable for short-term investments, fix-and-flip projects, or properties requiring rapid acquisition and renovation.

- ❖ **Seller Financing:** Seller financing allows property sellers to act as lenders by offering financing terms directly to buyers. This arrangement typically involves negotiating interest rates, repayment schedules, and down payment requirements agreed upon between the buyer and seller. Seller financing provides flexibility, streamlines transaction processes, and expands financing options for buyers with limited access to traditional mortgage loans.

- ❖ **Crowdfunding and Peer-to-Peer Lending:** Online platforms facilitate crowdfunding and peer-to-peer (P2P) lending opportunities for real estate investments, allowing multiple investors to pool funds and participate in fractional ownership of properties. Crowdfunding platforms offer diverse investment opportunities, transparency, and accessibility to accredited and non-accredited investors interested in passive real estate investments without direct property management responsibilities.

- ❖ **Home Equity Financing:** Homeowners can leverage existing home equity through home equity lines of credit (HELOCs) or cash-out refinancing to fund real estate investments. Home equity financing offers competitive interest rates, tax-deductible interest payments, and flexibility to access equity for property acquisitions, renovations, or portfolio expansion based on accumulated property equity and market value appreciation.

By exploring diverse funding options, including traditional mortgages and alternative financing methods, real estate investors can optimize capital deployment, mitigate financial risks, and capitalize on investment opportunities aligned with their investment objectives and financial strategies.

Understanding the nuances of each funding option enables investors to make informed decisions, negotiate favorable terms, and achieve sustainable growth and profitability in their real estate portfolios.

Securing Financing

Securing financing is a pivotal step in real estate investment, as it provides the capital necessary to acquire properties and execute investment strategies effectively. Whether you're purchasing residential, commercial, or investment properties, navigating the financing process requires thorough preparation, understanding of lender requirements, and strategic planning to optimize loan eligibility and terms. Securing financing involves evaluating various loan options, preparing comprehensive loan applications, and negotiating terms that align with your financial goals and investment objectives.

Preparing for Loan Applications

Preparing for loan applications begins with assessing your financial readiness and gathering essential documentation to demonstrate creditworthiness and repayment capacity to potential lenders. Key steps include:

- ❖ **Financial Assessment:** Evaluate your current financial situation, including income sources, savings, investments, and liabilities. Calculate your debt-to-income ratio (DTI) to determine your ability to manage additional debt payments and ensure affordability of mortgage payments relative to your income.

- ❖ **Credit Evaluation:** Obtain a copy of your credit report from major credit bureaus and review your credit score, payment history, and outstanding debts. Address any discrepancies or negative entries that may impact your creditworthiness and eligibility for favorable loan terms. Improving your credit score through timely debt repayment and reducing outstanding balances enhances your chances of securing competitive interest rates and loan approval.

- ❖ **Financial Documentation:** Gather necessary financial documents, including income verification (pay stubs, tax returns, W-2 forms), asset statements (bank statements, investment accounts), employment history, and identification documents (driver's license, passport). Organize documentation to support your loan application and provide lenders with accurate information to assess your financial stability and repayment capacity.

❖ **Down Payment and Reserves:** Save for a down payment, typically ranging from 3% to 20% of the property's purchase price, depending on loan type and lender requirements. Accumulate reserves to cover closing costs, prepaid expenses (property taxes, insurance), and potential unforeseen expenses to demonstrate financial preparedness and mitigate lender risk.

❖ **Prequalification and Preapproval:** Consider obtaining prequalification or preapproval from lenders to assess your borrowing capacity and streamline the loan application process. Prequalification provides an estimate of the loan amount you may qualify for based on initial financial information, while preapproval involves a comprehensive credit review and verification of financial documents to confirm loan eligibility and enhance offer credibility during property negotiations.

Understanding Loan Terms and Conditions

Understanding loan terms and conditions is essential for evaluating loan offers, comparing financing options, and selecting a loan structure that aligns with your investment strategy and financial objectives. Key components of loan terms and conditions include:

❖ **Interest Rates:** Evaluate fixed-rate and adjustable-rate mortgage (ARM) options to determine the initial interest rate, rate adjustments, and potential impact on monthly payments over the loan term. Fixed-rate mortgages offer stable payments and protection against interest rate fluctuations, while ARMs provide lower initial rates but involve periodic adjustments based on market indexes.

❖ **Loan Duration:** Consider loan duration, typically ranging from 15 to 30 years for residential mortgages, and assess the impact on total interest paid and monthly affordability. Shorter loan terms reduce overall interest costs but require higher monthly payments, while longer terms offer lower monthly payments but higher interest expenses over time.

❖ **Loan Fees and Closing Costs:** Review lender fees, origination charges, points (discount or origination points), and closing costs associated with loan processing and settlement. Negotiate with lenders to minimize fees and explore options for financing closing costs or incorporating costs into the loan amount to conserve cash reserves for property investments and renovations.

❖ **Loan Terms and Repayment Schedule:** Understand loan terms, repayment schedules, and amortization methods to calculate principal and interest payments accurately. Verify loan features such as prepayment penalties, balloon payments, and escrow accounts for property taxes and insurance to ensure compliance with lender requirements and maintain financial stability throughout the loan term.

❖ **Loan Conditions and Contingencies:** Review loan conditions, contingencies, and underwriting requirements to meet lender stipulations for loan approval. Address lender requests for additional documentation, property appraisals, and title insurance to facilitate timely loan processing and minimize delays in property acquisition and closing.

By preparing diligently for loan applications, understanding loan terms and conditions, and collaborating effectively with lenders, real estate investors can navigate the financing process confidently and secure funding solutions that support their investment goals and enhance portfolio growth. Comprehensive preparation, financial transparency, and proactive communication with lenders foster productive partnerships and facilitate successful real estate transactions tailored to achieve long-term financial success and investment profitability.

Creative Financing Strategies

Creative financing strategies in real estate provide innovative solutions for acquiring properties and optimizing investment opportunities beyond traditional mortgage loans. These strategies leverage alternative funding sources, collaborative partnerships, and customized financing arrangements to overcome financing challenges, enhance investment flexibility, and maximize returns. Two prominent creative financing strategies include owner financing and partnering/syndication.

Owner Financing

Owner financing, also known as seller financing or seller carryback, involves the property seller acting as the lender to facilitate the sale of the property. In owner financing arrangements, the seller extends a loan to the buyer for a portion or the entire purchase price, which the buyer repays through agreed-upon terms, including interest rates, repayment schedules, and loan duration.

This financing method benefits both buyers and sellers by:

- ❖ **Flexible Terms:** Negotiating flexible loan terms, such as lower down payments, competitive interest rates, and extended repayment periods, which may appeal to buyers unable to secure traditional mortgage financing due to credit challenges or insufficient down payment funds.

- ❖ **Streamlined Process:** Simplifying transaction processes and reducing closing costs by eliminating or minimizing lender fees, loan origination charges, and third-party underwriting requirements typically associated with conventional mortgages.

- ❖ **Property Accessibility:** Facilitating property acquisitions for buyers by offering alternative financing options and expediting purchase agreements, accelerating property transactions without prolonged mortgage approval timelines or stringent qualification criteria.

For sellers, owner financing presents opportunities to:

- ❖ **Generate Passive Income:** Earn interest income through installment payments, providing ongoing cash flow and potentially higher returns compared to traditional investment vehicles or outright property sales.

- ❖ **Expand Buyer Pool:** Attract a broader range of potential buyers, including investors, first-time homebuyers, or individuals facing challenges obtaining mortgage financing, thereby increasing marketability and facilitating property sales in competitive real estate markets.

❖ **Negotiate Favorable Terms:** Negotiate favorable sales terms, such as higher purchase prices, shorter closing periods, and seller-friendly contract provisions, enhancing negotiation leverage and optimizing financial outcomes from property transactions.

Owner financing arrangements typically involve legal agreements, promissory notes, and recorded liens to secure repayment obligations and protect both parties' interests throughout the loan term. Engaging legal counsel and financial advisors ensures compliance with regulatory requirements, facilitates transparent negotiations, and mitigates risks associated with seller financing transactions.

Partnering and Syndication

Partnering and syndication strategies enable real estate investors to pool financial resources, expertise, and resources with multiple investors or partners to collectively finance and manage investment properties. These collaborative arrangements combine individual strengths, diversify investment risks, and capitalize on shared opportunities to achieve mutual investment goals and maximize portfolio growth.

Key components of partnering and syndication include:

- ❖ **Joint Ventures:** Forming joint venture partnerships with individuals or entities to combine capital contributions, industry knowledge, and operational expertise for acquiring, managing, and improving real estate properties. Joint ventures distribute ownership stakes, responsibilities, and profits based on agreed-upon terms outlined in partnership agreements and operating agreements.

- ❖ **Limited Liability Companies (LLCs):** Establishing LLC structures to organize syndicated investments, allowing multiple investors (members) to contribute equity capital and share ownership interests in real estate assets. LLCs provide liability protection, operational flexibility, and governance frameworks for managing investments, distributing profits, and navigating legal and regulatory compliance requirements.

❖ **Real Estate Syndication:** Implementing real estate syndication models, such as private placements or real estate investment trusts (REITs), to pool funds from accredited investors and institutional partners for acquiring income-producing properties, development projects, or distressed assets. Syndicators act as sponsors or general partners responsible for sourcing deals, managing investments, and overseeing asset performance, while investors participate as limited partners or shareholders to access diversified real estate portfolios and potential investment returns.

Partnering and syndication strategies require comprehensive due diligence, investor relations management, and legal structuring to align investor expectations, distribute financial risks, and optimize returns on real estate investments. Engaging experienced professionals, including real estate attorneys, financial advisors, and syndication specialists, facilitates strategic planning, regulatory compliance, and operational execution for successful partnership formations and syndicated investment ventures.

In conclusion, creative financing strategies such as owner financing and partnering/syndication offer alternative funding solutions and collaborative opportunities for real estate investors to acquire properties, optimize investment capital, and achieve long-term financial objectives. By leveraging innovative financing approaches, investors can navigate market dynamics, capitalize on investment opportunities, and enhance portfolio diversification while mitigating risks and maximizing returns in the competitive real estate industry.

Leveraging Equity

Leveraging equity in real estate involves utilizing the value of owned properties to access capital for investment opportunities, debt consolidation, home improvements, or other financial needs. This strategy allows property owners to unlock the equity accumulated in their homes or investment properties through various financial instruments, including home equity loans, lines of credit, and using equity in other properties.

Home Equity Loans and Lines of Credit

Home equity loans and lines of credit (HELOCs) are common methods to leverage equity in primary residences or second homes, providing homeowners with access to funds based on the difference between the property's market value and outstanding mortgage balance.

- ❖ **Home Equity Loans:** Home equity loans offer lump-sum disbursements with fixed interest rates and predictable monthly payments over a specified term, typically ranging from 5 to 30 years. Borrowers use home equity loans to finance large expenses, such as home renovations, educational expenses, or debt consolidation, leveraging property equity as collateral to secure favorable loan terms and lower interest rates compared to unsecured personal loans.

❖ **Home Equity Lines of Credit (HELOCs):** HELOCs function as revolving lines of credit that allow homeowners to borrow against available equity, access funds as needed, and repay outstanding balances with variable interest rates based on market indexes. HELOCs offer flexibility for ongoing expenses, emergency funds, or investment opportunities, enabling borrowers to withdraw funds, make interest-only payments during the draw period, and manage cash flow based on fluctuating financial needs and market conditions.

Both home equity loans and HELOCs require equity verification, creditworthiness assessment, and appraisal of property value to determine maximum borrowing limits, loan-to-value (LTV) ratios, and eligibility criteria set by lenders. Borrowers should compare loan offers, review disclosure statements, and evaluate repayment obligations, including principal repayment and interest accrual, to align with financial goals and budgetary considerations.

Using Equity in Other Properties

Utilizing equity in other properties involves leveraging owned real estate assets, including residential or commercial properties, to access capital for additional investments, property acquisitions, or business ventures. Equity extraction strategies include:

- ❖ **Cash-Out Refinancing:** Cash-out refinancing allows property owners to replace existing mortgage loans with new loans that exceed the current mortgage balance, enabling borrowers to withdraw equity in cash based on updated property appraisals and refinancing terms. Cash-out refinancing offers fixed or adjustable interest rates, extended loan terms, and potential tax advantages for deducting mortgage interest payments, providing liquidity for real estate investments or personal financial goals.

- ❖ **Cross-Collateralization:** Cross-collateralization involves pledging equity from multiple properties as collateral to secure financing for new acquisitions, expansion projects, or debt consolidation purposes. Lenders evaluate combined property values, loan-to-value ratios, and borrower creditworthiness to structure cross-collateralized loans or lines of credit, optimizing equity utilization and leveraging diverse real estate portfolios to mitigate financial risks and maximize borrowing capacity.

❖ **Equity Sharing:** Equity sharing agreements enable property owners to partner with investors or equity partners to access capital in exchange for shared ownership interests or profit-sharing arrangements in real estate assets. Equity partners contribute funds for property acquisitions, renovations, or development projects, leveraging property equity as collateral to achieve mutual investment objectives, enhance property values, and generate returns through rental income, property appreciation, or resale proceeds.

Effective equity leveraging strategies require strategic planning, financial discipline, and risk management to optimize investment opportunities, minimize borrowing costs, and maximize returns on real estate assets. Property owners should consult with mortgage lenders, financial advisors, and legal professionals to explore financing options, evaluate tax implications, and implement customized equity leveraging strategies aligned with long-term financial objectives and portfolio growth initiatives in the competitive real estate market.

Real Estate Investment Strategies

Real estate investment strategies encompass diverse approaches and techniques tailored to achieve specific financial goals, risk profiles, and investment horizons. Two prominent strategies include buy and hold investments and property flipping, each offering distinct advantages, challenges, and potential returns in the dynamic real estate market.

Buy and Hold Investments

Buy and hold investing involves acquiring properties with the intention of holding them over an extended period, typically years or decades, to generate rental income, achieve long-term appreciation, and build equity accumulation. This strategy emphasizes passive income streams, property value appreciation, and portfolio diversification for sustainable wealth creation and retirement planning.

❖ **Income Generation:** Buy and hold investors generate steady cash flow through rental income from residential, commercial, or multi-family properties, leveraging tenant occupancy and lease agreements to cover mortgage payments, property maintenance costs, and operational expenses. Positive cash flow strengthens financial stability, supports property management efforts, and enhances portfolio resilience against market fluctuations and economic cycles.

❖ **Long-Term Appreciation:** Capitalizing on property appreciation potential, buy and hold investors benefit from long-term market trends, economic growth, and demographic shifts influencing real estate values. Holding properties over extended periods allows investors to maximize equity growth, capitalize on tax-deferred appreciation, and leverage property improvements or market upgrades to enhance asset values and overall investment returns.

- ❖ **Equity Buildup:** Leveraging mortgage amortization, principal payments, and property value appreciation, buy and hold investors accumulate equity over time, expanding borrowing capacity, and accessing liquidity for additional property acquisitions, renovations, or portfolio diversification strategies. Equity buildup provides financial leverage, supports debt reduction strategies, and enhances net worth through strategic real estate investments and asset management practices.

Challenges associated with buy and hold investments include property maintenance responsibilities, tenant management, vacancy risks, and potential economic downturns impacting rental demand and cash flow stability. Mitigating risks through proactive property management, contingency planning, and diversifying investment portfolios minimizes vulnerabilities and safeguards long-term investment objectives in the competitive real estate landscape.

Property Flipping

Property flipping, or fix-and-flip investing, involves purchasing distressed or undervalued properties, renovating or improving them, and reselling for profit within a relatively short timeframe, typically months or a few years. This strategy focuses on capitalizing on property market inefficiencies, renovation opportunities, and market demand for updated or revitalized properties.

- ❖ **Profit Potential:** Flipping properties allows investors to realize short-term profits through strategic renovations, aesthetic enhancements, and value-added improvements that appeal to prospective buyers or tenants. Profiting from property appreciation and market demand, flippers optimize resale values, maximize investment returns, and capitalize on favorable market conditions and property market cycles.

- **Renovation Expertise:** Expertise in property renovation, construction management, and project planning enables flippers to execute cost-effective renovations, streamline construction timelines, and enhance property aesthetics, functionality, and marketability. Leveraging renovation skills and industry relationships optimizes project outcomes, minimizes renovation costs, and accelerates property turnaround for resale or rental occupancy.

- **Market Timing:** Effective market analysis, trend forecasting, and property valuation inform strategic buying decisions, renovation plans, and resale timing to capitalize on market appreciation, buyer demand, and competitive pricing strategies. Monitoring local market conditions, economic indicators, and consumer preferences guides flippers in identifying profitable investment opportunities and optimizing property investment performance.

Despite potential profitability, property flipping involves inherent risks, including renovation budget overruns, project delays, market volatility, and regulatory compliance challenges. Implementing thorough due diligence, financial planning, and risk management strategies mitigates investment risks, enhances project profitability, and supports sustainable growth in the competitive real estate market.

In summary, real estate investment strategies such as buy and hold investments and property flipping offer distinct pathways to achieve financial goals, generate investment income, and build wealth through strategic property acquisitions, management practices, and market opportunities. By aligning investment strategies with personal objectives, risk tolerance, and market dynamics, investors can navigate real estate markets effectively, optimize investment returns, and achieve long-term financial success in an evolving economic environment.

Investing in Rental Properties

Investing in rental properties is a strategic approach to generating passive income, building wealth through real estate appreciation, and diversifying investment portfolios. Successful rental property investments require careful selection of profitable properties, effective tenant management, and proactive rental income management to optimize cash flow and achieve long-term financial objectives.

Selecting Profitable Rental Properties

Selecting profitable rental properties involves evaluating key factors that influence investment performance, rental income potential, and property appreciation over time. Considerations include:

- ❖ **Location and Market Demand:** Identify neighborhoods with strong rental demand, low vacancy rates, and potential for property appreciation based on demographic trends, employment opportunities, and neighborhood amenities (schools, transportation, retail centers). Analyze local market dynamics, rental market trends, and economic indicators to assess investment viability and rental income potential.

❖ **Property Condition and Potential Renovations:** Evaluate property condition, structural integrity, and renovation opportunities to enhance property value, attract quality tenants, and maximize rental income. Prioritize properties requiring cosmetic upgrades or value-added improvements (kitchen renovations, bathroom remodels, energy-efficient upgrades) that align with market preferences and rental property standards.

❖ **Financial Analysis and Investment Returns:** Conduct comprehensive financial analysis, including cash flow projections, cap rate calculations, and return on investment (ROI) metrics, to assess profitability and investment feasibility. Evaluate purchase price relative to rental income potential, operating expenses (property taxes, insurance, maintenance), financing costs, and anticipated vacancy rates to determine net operating income (NOI) and cash-on-cash returns.

❖ **Tenant Profile and Screening Process:** Implement rigorous tenant screening criteria, including credit checks, rental history verification, employment verification, and criminal background checks, to identify reliable tenants capable of meeting lease obligations and maintaining property integrity. Establish clear tenant qualification standards, lease agreements, and rental policies to mitigate tenant-related risks and ensure sustainable rental income streams.

- ❖ **Property Management Considerations:** Evaluate property management options, whether self-managing or hiring professional property management services, to oversee tenant relations, property maintenance, rent collection, and compliance with rental regulations. Implement proactive maintenance practices, routine property inspections, and responsive tenant communication to uphold property value, tenant satisfaction, and regulatory compliance.

Managing Tenants and Rental Income

Managing tenants and rental income requires proactive communication, lease enforcement, financial oversight, and property maintenance to optimize occupancy rates, rental income stability, and tenant retention. Key management strategies include:

- ❖ **Lease Administration and Legal Compliance:** Administer lease agreements outlining rental terms, tenant responsibilities, maintenance protocols, and dispute resolution procedures in accordance with local rental laws and regulatory requirements. Maintain accurate lease records, lease renewals, and rent adjustments to ensure legal compliance, mitigate landlord-tenant disputes, and protect investment interests.

- ❖ **Rent Collection and Financial Reporting:** Implement efficient rent collection methods, such as online payment platforms or automated rent deposits, to streamline payment processing, reduce delinquency rates, and maintain consistent cash flow. Monitor rental income, expense tracking, and financial performance through detailed accounting practices, budgeting tools, and periodic financial reporting to assess property profitability and inform investment decisions.

❖ **Tenant Relations and Communication:** Foster positive tenant relations through proactive communication, responsive maintenance requests, and tenant-centric policies that promote tenant satisfaction, retention, and property upkeep. Address tenant concerns promptly, maintain open communication channels, and cultivate respectful landlord-tenant relationships to minimize turnover rates and maximize tenant longevity.

❖ **Maintenance and Property Upkeep:** Prioritize property maintenance, routine inspections, and preventive repairs to preserve property value, address maintenance issues promptly, and comply with health, safety, and habitability standards. Schedule regular property inspections, coordinate maintenance services, and invest in property improvements to enhance tenant living conditions, attract prospective renters, and mitigate property depreciation risks.

❖ **Risk Management and Legal Protection:** Implement risk management strategies, including landlord insurance coverage, property liability protection, and lease provisions addressing property damage, insurance requirements, and tenant responsibilities. Stay informed about landlord-tenant laws, eviction procedures, fair housing regulations, and local rental ordinances to safeguard legal interests, enforce lease agreements, and resolve tenancy disputes effectively.

By selecting profitable rental properties based on market analysis, financial feasibility, and tenant management strategies, real estate investors can optimize rental income, mitigate investment risks, and achieve long-term financial success through strategic property acquisitions and effective property management practices. Continuous monitoring of market trends, tenant dynamics, and operational efficiencies ensures proactive investment management, sustainable rental income growth, and resilience in the competitive rental property market.

Commercial Real Estate Investments

Investing in commercial real estate encompasses a range of property types and investment opportunities tailored to business operations, income generation, and portfolio diversification. Understanding the types of commercial properties and evaluating investment opportunities are essential for identifying profitable ventures and achieving long-term financial objectives in the competitive commercial real estate market.

Types of Commercial Properties

Commercial properties encompass diverse asset classes that cater to various industries, tenant requirements, and investment strategies. Key types of commercial properties include:

- ❖ **Office Buildings:** Office buildings accommodate professional services, corporate headquarters, and business operations, ranging from small office suites to high-rise complexes in urban centers or suburban business parks. Investment considerations include location accessibility, tenant demand from corporate tenants or startups, lease terms (gross lease, net lease), and technological infrastructure to support modern workplace environments.

❖ **Retail Centers:** Retail centers encompass shopping malls, strip malls, and standalone retail spaces leased to retailers, restaurants, and service providers. Investment factors include location visibility, demographic trends, tenant mix (anchor tenants, national brands, local businesses), foot traffic patterns, and lease structures (percentage rent, triple net lease) influencing rental income and tenant stability.

❖ **Industrial Properties:** Industrial properties include warehouses, distribution centers, manufacturing facilities, and logistics hubs essential for supply chain management, storage, and product distribution. Investment considerations focus on proximity to transportation hubs (airports, highways, ports), industrial zoning regulations, tenant creditworthiness (e-commerce, logistics companies), building specifications (clear height, loading docks), and lease terms (tenant improvements, lease duration) affecting operational efficiencies and asset performance.

❖ **Multifamily Properties:** Multifamily properties encompass apartment buildings, condominiums, and residential complexes offering rental housing options to tenants. Investment advantages include recurring rental income, occupancy rates, tenant retention, and property amenities (parking, recreational facilities). Evaluate market demand, rental market trends, property management efficiencies, and tenant demographics (young professionals, families, retirees) to optimize cash flow, property valuation, and long-term investment returns.

❖ **Hospitality Properties:** Hospitality properties include hotels, resorts, and vacation rentals catering to transient guests, tourists, and business travelers seeking short-term accommodations. Investment considerations encompass location (tourist destinations, business districts), hotel classification (limited service, full-service), occupancy rates, revenue per available room (RevPAR), operating expenses (staffing, maintenance), and market demand fluctuations impacting hospitality industry performance and profitability.

❖ **Special Purpose Properties:** Special purpose properties encompass unique assets, such as healthcare facilities (hospitals, medical offices), educational institutions (schools, universities), religious facilities (churches, synagogues), and recreational properties (golf courses, sports complexes). Investment strategies focus on tenant niche markets, regulatory compliance (healthcare regulations, zoning ordinances), lease agreements (long-term leases, specialized tenant improvements), and community impact influencing property valuation and operational sustainability.

Evaluating Commercial Investment Opportunities

Evaluating commercial investment opportunities requires comprehensive due diligence, financial analysis, and market research to assess property performance, investment risks, and potential returns. Key evaluation criteria include:

- **Market Analysis:** Conduct thorough market research to identify local economic trends, demographic shifts, supply-demand dynamics, and competitive landscape affecting commercial property values, rental rates, and tenant demand. Analyze market vacancy rates, absorption rates, and market forecasts to gauge investment feasibility and market positioning relative to competing properties.

- **Financial Feasibility:** Evaluate financial metrics, including net operating income (NOI), capitalization rate (cap rate), cash-on-cash return, and internal rate of return (IRR), to quantify investment returns, assess property profitability, and compare investment opportunities. Calculate operating expenses, property taxes, insurance costs, and financing terms (loan amortization, interest rates) to determine cash flow projections and investment viability based on risk-adjusted return expectations.

- ❖ **Property Condition and Due Diligence:** Conduct property inspections, environmental assessments, and structural evaluations to assess building condition, compliance with building codes, and potential repair or renovation costs. Review lease agreements, tenant credit profiles, lease expiration schedules, and tenant improvement allowances to understand tenant stability, lease rollover risks, and capital expenditure requirements affecting property maintenance and investment performance.

- ❖ **Legal and Regulatory Considerations:** Navigate legal complexities, zoning ordinances, land use restrictions, and regulatory compliance requirements governing commercial property transactions. Consult with legal advisors, real estate professionals, and municipal authorities to mitigate legal risks, address property title issues, and ensure transactional integrity throughout due diligence and closing processes.

❖ **Exit Strategies and Portfolio Alignment:** Develop exit strategies, including property disposition plans, refinancing options, and portfolio diversification strategies aligned with investment objectives, market cycles, and investor liquidity preferences. Evaluate portfolio alignment, risk tolerance, and asset allocation strategies to optimize investment portfolio growth, mitigate concentration risks, and capitalize on emerging market opportunities within the commercial real estate sector.

By understanding the nuances of commercial property types, conducting rigorous investment evaluations, and leveraging strategic insights into market dynamics and financial performance metrics, real estate investors can identify lucrative investment opportunities, optimize asset management strategies, and achieve sustainable growth and profitability in the dynamic commercial real estate market landscape.

Real Estate Investment Trusts (REITs)

Real Estate Investment Trusts (REITs) are specialized investment vehicles that allow individuals to invest in real estate assets without directly owning or managing properties. REITs pool capital from investors to acquire, manage, and finance income-producing properties, providing investors with access to diversified real estate portfolios and potential income streams through dividends and capital appreciation.

Understanding REITs

REITs operate under specific regulatory guidelines and tax considerations established by governments to qualify for favorable tax treatment. Key characteristics of REITs include:

- ❖ **Income-Generating Assets:** REITs invest in a variety of real estate sectors, including commercial properties (office buildings, retail centers, industrial facilities), residential properties (apartment complexes, condominiums), healthcare facilities (hospitals, medical offices), and specialized properties (hotels, self-storage units). By diversifying property holdings, REITs mitigate investment risks and leverage economies of scale to optimize property management efficiencies and rental income generation.

- ❖ **Dividend Distribution:** REITs distribute a significant portion of taxable income to shareholders in the form of dividends, typically quarterly or semi-annually. Dividend payments provide investors with regular income streams and potential tax advantages, as REITs are required to distribute at least 90% of taxable income to shareholders to maintain tax-exempt status and avoid corporate income taxes.

❖ **Liquidity and Accessibility:** REIT shares trade on major stock exchanges similar to publicly traded companies, offering investors liquidity and flexibility to buy, sell, or exchange shares based on market conditions and investment preferences. Unlike direct real estate investments requiring substantial capital, REIT investments allow investors to participate in real estate markets with lower entry costs and portfolio diversification benefits.

❖ **Regulatory Compliance:** REITs must adhere to regulatory requirements, including asset diversification rules, income distribution mandates, and shareholder ownership limits, to qualify as tax-advantaged investment entities. Compliance with Securities and Exchange Commission (SEC) regulations, financial reporting standards, and governance practices ensures transparency, investor protection, and operational integrity within the REIT industry.

Benefits of Investing in REITs

Investing in REITs offers several potential benefits for individual investors seeking exposure to real estate markets and income-generating assets:

- ❖ **Diversification:** REITs provide access to diversified real estate portfolios across multiple property sectors, geographic regions, and tenant industries, reducing investment concentration risk and enhancing portfolio stability through income diversification and asset allocation strategies.

- ❖ **Income Generation:** REITs generate consistent dividend income derived from rental income, lease payments, and property operations, offering investors predictable cash flow streams and potential inflation-hedging benefits compared to fixed-income investments or dividend-paying stocks.

- **Capital Appreciation:** REITs may experience capital appreciation based on property value appreciation, market demand trends, and portfolio management strategies implemented by REIT managers to enhance property performance, optimize asset values, and capitalize on market opportunities.

- **Accessibility and Liquidity:** REIT shares trade on public exchanges, providing investors with liquidity to buy or sell shares based on market conditions, portfolio rebalancing needs, or investment goals without the liquidity constraints associated with direct real estate investments.

- **Tax Advantages:** REITs qualify for pass-through tax treatment, allowing investors to defer taxation on distributed dividends and potentially reduce overall tax liabilities through deductions for depreciation expenses, operating expenses, and mortgage interest payments incurred by REITs.

Risks of Investing in REITs

While REITs offer compelling benefits, investors should consider potential risks associated with REIT investments:

- ❖ **Market Risks:** REITs are sensitive to real estate market fluctuations, economic cycles, interest rate movements, and supply-demand dynamics impacting property values, rental income, and investment returns. Market volatility may affect REIT share prices, dividend yields, and investor sentiment in response to macroeconomic conditions and industry-specific challenges.

- ❖ **Interest Rate Risk:** REITs may be susceptible to interest rate risk, as rising interest rates could increase borrowing costs for REITs, reduce profitability margins, and affect property valuations, potentially leading to lower dividend distributions and share price volatility.

❖ **Sector-Specific Risks:** Different real estate sectors within REIT portfolios, such as retail, hospitality, or office properties, face sector-specific risks, including changing consumer preferences, tenant turnover, lease expirations, and regulatory changes impacting property operations and financial performance.

❖ **Leverage and Financial Risk:** Some REITs utilize leverage (debt financing) to acquire properties and expand portfolios, increasing financial leverage ratios, interest expense obligations, and sensitivity to credit market conditions. High leverage levels may amplify investment risks during economic downturns or adverse market conditions affecting REIT liquidity and debt repayment capabilities.

❖ **Management and Operational Risks:** REIT performance is influenced by management decisions, property management effectiveness, tenant relations, operational efficiencies, and adherence to strategic business plans aimed at maximizing property occupancy rates, rental income growth, and asset value appreciation.

Investors should conduct thorough due diligence, assess risk tolerance, and consult with financial advisors to evaluate REIT investment opportunities, understand potential risks, and align investment strategies with long-term financial goals and portfolio objectives. By balancing potential rewards with inherent risks, investors can make informed decisions to optimize real estate exposure, income generation, and wealth preservation through diversified REIT investments in the global real estate marketplace.

Property Management Best Practices

Effective property management is crucial for maximizing property value, tenant satisfaction, and investment returns in real estate. Implementing best practices in maintenance and repairs, as well as knowing when to hire professional property managers, ensures operational efficiency, tenant retention, and asset preservation.

Maintenance and Repairs

Maintenance and repair strategies are integral to maintaining property condition, tenant satisfaction, and overall investment performance:

- ❖ **Proactive Maintenance Planning:** Develop a proactive maintenance schedule to address routine inspections, preventive maintenance tasks, and seasonal upkeep to preserve property functionality, safety, and aesthetic appeal. Schedule regular HVAC servicing, plumbing inspections, roof inspections, and landscaping maintenance to mitigate potential property damage, reduce emergency repair costs, and enhance tenant satisfaction through well-maintained living or working environments.

❖ **Prompt Response to Maintenance Requests:** Establish responsive communication channels and maintenance request protocols to address tenant inquiries, repair requests, and property maintenance issues promptly. Implement an online maintenance portal or tenant communication platform to streamline service requests, prioritize urgent repairs, and ensure timely resolution of maintenance issues to minimize tenant inconvenience and uphold property management standards.

❖ **Quality Control and Vendor Management:** Partner with reputable contractors, maintenance professionals, and service providers capable of delivering quality workmanship, timely repairs, and cost-effective solutions aligned with property maintenance budgets and operational objectives. Conduct vendor performance reviews, negotiate service contracts, and enforce service level agreements to maintain service quality standards, manage vendor relationships, and optimize operational efficiencies in property management practices.

- ❖ **Budgeting and Capital Expenditure Planning:** Allocate sufficient funds for routine maintenance expenses, capital improvements, and emergency repairs through proactive budget planning and capital expenditure forecasts. Prioritize budget allocations for property upgrades, major systems replacements (HVAC systems, roofing), and infrastructure enhancements to enhance property value, extend asset lifespan, and minimize long-term maintenance costs impacting property operating expenses and investment profitability.

❖ **Tenant Communication and Education:** Educate tenants on property maintenance responsibilities, emergency procedures, and tenant obligations outlined in lease agreements to promote proactive property care, tenant cooperation, and adherence to property rules and regulations. Foster open communication channels, distribute maintenance guidelines, and encourage tenant feedback to address maintenance concerns promptly, enhance tenant satisfaction, and maintain positive landlord-tenant relationships conducive to long-term lease renewals and tenant retention strategies.

Hiring Professional Property Managers

Knowing when to hire professional property managers provides expertise, operational oversight, and strategic management support to optimize property performance and investor returns:

- ❖ **Expertise in Property Operations:** Professional property managers possess industry knowledge, market insights, and operational expertise to navigate complex property management challenges, regulatory compliance requirements, and tenant relations effectively. Leverage professional property management services to implement best practices, streamline operational workflows, and enhance property value through proactive management strategies tailored to investor objectives and property performance goals.

- **Tenant Acquisition and Retention:** Utilize property managers' marketing expertise, tenant screening processes, and leasing strategies to attract qualified tenants, minimize vacancy rates, and optimize rental income generation. Property managers conduct thorough tenant screenings, negotiate lease agreements, enforce lease terms, and implement tenant retention programs to foster tenant satisfaction, reduce turnover costs, and sustain occupancy levels contributing to stable cash flow and investment profitability.

- **Financial Management and Reporting:** Outsource financial management responsibilities to property managers proficient in budget planning, rent collection, expense management, and financial reporting to monitor property performance, track income and expenses, and analyze financial metrics impacting investment returns. Property managers prepare detailed financial statements, conduct rent reviews, and implement cost-saving initiatives to optimize property profitability, maximize cash flow, and facilitate informed decision-making aligned with investor objectives and financial goals.

- **Maintenance and Property Care:** Delegate maintenance supervision, repair coordination, and property upkeep responsibilities to property managers overseeing day-to-day operations, emergency response protocols, and vendor management to maintain property condition, ensure regulatory compliance, and minimize operational disruptions impacting tenant satisfaction and property performance metrics.

- ❖ **Risk Management and Legal Compliance:** Rely on property managers to navigate legal complexities, regulatory changes, and risk management challenges affecting property investments, lease agreements, and tenant relations. Property managers enforce lease provisions, adhere to fair housing regulations, and mitigate liability risks through proactive legal guidance, compliance monitoring, and dispute resolution strategies to protect investor interests, uphold property values, and ensure operational integrity within the competitive real estate market.

By implementing property management best practices, prioritizing maintenance and repairs, and considering professional property management services, real estate investors can optimize property performance, tenant satisfaction, and investment returns while mitigating operational risks and achieving long-term success in property ownership and management endeavors.

Tax Planning and Real Estate

Tax planning in real estate is essential for optimizing financial outcomes, maximizing tax benefits, and minimizing liabilities associated with property ownership, rental income, and investment transactions. Understanding real estate taxes, tax benefits, and deductions enables investors to leverage tax-efficient strategies, comply with regulatory requirements, and enhance overall investment profitability within the complex tax landscape of real estate investments.

Understanding Real Estate Taxes

Real estate taxes encompass various tax obligations, assessments, and regulatory requirements applicable to property ownership, rental income generation, and investment transactions:

- ❖ **Property Taxes:** Property taxes are levied annually by local governments based on property assessments and millage rates, funding public services, schools, and infrastructure improvements within the property's jurisdiction. Property tax assessments consider property value assessments, taxable assessments, and applicable tax rates affecting annual property tax liabilities for residential, commercial, and industrial properties.

❖ **Income Taxes on Rental Income:** Rental income generated from investment properties is subject to federal and state income taxes, including rental income received from residential, commercial, or multifamily properties. Investors report rental income and expenses on annual tax returns, deducting allowable expenses (mortgage interest, property taxes, maintenance costs) from rental income to calculate taxable net rental income subject to marginal tax rates and applicable tax deductions.

- ❖ **Capital Gains Taxes:** Capital gains taxes apply to profits realized from the sale or disposition of investment properties held for more than one year, subject to long-term capital gains tax rates based on property appreciation, adjusted basis, and holding period. Investors may offset capital gains with capital losses, utilize 1031 exchanges for tax-deferred reinvestment, or qualify for capital gains tax exclusions (primary residence exemption) to mitigate taxable gains from property sales and optimize investment returns.

- ❖ **Depreciation Deductions:** Real estate investors benefit from depreciation deductions allowing annual deductions for property depreciation expenses based on property type (residential or commercial), recovery periods, and depreciation methods (straight-line depreciation, accelerated depreciation). Depreciation deductions reduce taxable rental income, lower tax liabilities, and improve cash flow by allocating depreciation expenses over property useful life for tax planning purposes.

❖ **1031 Exchange Benefits:** Section 1031 exchanges facilitate tax-deferred exchanges of like-kind investment properties, allowing investors to defer capital gains taxes on property sales by reinvesting sale proceeds into qualifying replacement properties within specified timelines and compliance with exchange requirements. 1031 exchanges enable portfolio diversification, asset consolidation, and tax-efficient wealth preservation strategies without immediate tax consequences upon property disposition.

Tax Benefits and Deductions

Real estate investments offer various tax benefits and deductions that enhance investment profitability and support long-term wealth accumulation strategies:

- ❖ **Mortgage Interest Deductions:** Investors deduct mortgage interest payments on investment property loans, including interest paid on mortgage loans, home equity lines of credit (HELOCs), and refinanced mortgages used to finance property acquisitions, improvements, or capital expenditures. Mortgage interest deductions reduce taxable rental income, lower effective tax rates, and improve cash flow by offsetting interest expenses against rental income for tax purposes.

- ❖ **Operating Expenses Deductions:** Deductible operating expenses include property management fees, maintenance costs, repairs, utilities, insurance premiums, property taxes, and administrative expenses incurred in property operations and management. Investors deduct allowable expenses from rental income to calculate taxable net operating income subject to federal and state income taxes, reducing tax liabilities and optimizing cash flow through expense management and budget planning strategies.

❖ **Passive Activity Losses:** Real estate investors may offset passive activity losses (PALs) against passive income generated from rental activities, partnerships, or real estate investments, subject to passive activity loss rules and income limitations. PAL deductions reduce taxable income, mitigate tax liabilities, and optimize tax efficiency by utilizing passive losses to offset taxable gains and optimize overall investment portfolio performance through passive income tax planning strategies.

❖ **Section 179 Deductions:** Section 179 deductions allow immediate expensing of qualified real property improvements, leasehold improvements, and capital expenditures, accelerating depreciation deductions and reducing taxable income for real estate investors. Investors utilize Section 179 deductions to deduct eligible property improvement costs, enhance property value, and leverage tax savings to reinvest in property upgrades, renovations, or capital improvement projects benefiting investment returns and property appreciation.

❖ **Tax Credits and Incentives:** Utilize federal and state tax credits, incentives, and deductions available for energy-efficient property improvements, historic rehabilitation projects, low-income housing developments, and affordable housing initiatives promoting sustainable development, environmental stewardship, and community revitalization efforts. Tax credits and incentives reduce tax liabilities, offset project costs, and encourage real estate investments aligned with regulatory compliance, social responsibility, and economic development objectives benefiting investors and local communities.

By understanding real estate taxes, leveraging tax benefits, and optimizing tax deductions through strategic tax planning, real estate investors maximize investment returns, minimize tax liabilities, and achieve long-term financial objectives in the competitive real estate market. Consult with tax advisors, accountants, and legal professionals to implement tax-efficient strategies, navigate tax complexities, and capitalize on tax-saving opportunities aligned with investment goals and financial priorities within the evolving regulatory landscape of real estate taxation.

Building and Diversifying Your Portfolio

Building a robust real estate portfolio involves strategic planning, disciplined investment strategies, and diversification across property types and locations to optimize long-term growth, mitigate investment risks, and achieve diversified income streams. Implementing long-term growth strategies and diversification principles ensures portfolio resilience, capital appreciation, and sustainable investment performance in the dynamic real estate market landscape.

Long-term Growth Strategies

- ❖ **Strategic Property Selection:** Conduct comprehensive market research and due diligence to identify investment opportunities aligned with long-term growth objectives, market trends, and economic indicators influencing property values, rental demand, and investment returns. Evaluate property fundamentals, growth potential, and investment feasibility criteria (location, property condition, tenant demographics) to prioritize property acquisitions supporting portfolio expansion and capital appreciation strategies.

❖ **Value-Add Investments:** Implement value-add investment strategies through property renovations, capital improvements, and repositioning initiatives to enhance property value, optimize rental income potential, and differentiate properties within competitive markets. Execute cost-effective upgrades (kitchen remodels, energy-efficient enhancements) to attract quality tenants, increase property desirability, and maximize return on investment (ROI) through value enhancement strategies supporting long-term portfolio growth objectives.

- **Portfolio Diversification:** Diversify portfolio holdings across different real estate sectors (residential, commercial, industrial), property types (single-family homes, multifamily apartments, office buildings), and geographic locations (urban, suburban, rural markets) to mitigate sector-specific risks, market fluctuations, and economic cycles impacting investment performance. Allocate resources strategically across diversified assets, leverage economies of scale, and capitalize on market opportunities to optimize portfolio diversification benefits, income stability, and asset allocation strategies promoting long-term growth and risk management.

- **Risk Management Strategies:** Implement risk management strategies, including portfolio diversification, asset allocation adjustments, and investment hedging techniques (insurance coverage, lease diversification), to mitigate investment risks, protect capital investments, and safeguard portfolio value against unforeseen market volatility, tenant turnover, or economic downturns affecting real estate market conditions. Monitor portfolio performance, conduct stress testing scenarios, and adjust investment strategies based on risk tolerance, market dynamics, and macroeconomic factors influencing investment outcomes and portfolio resilience.

Diversifying Across Property Types and Locations

❖ **Property Type Diversification:** Diversify across property types (residential, commercial, industrial) to leverage sector-specific opportunities, rental income diversification, and market demand dynamics across different real estate asset classes. Allocate investments across residential properties offering stable rental income, commercial properties generating higher yields, and industrial properties supporting logistics and supply chain sectors to optimize portfolio returns and sector-specific investment strategies aligned with investor objectives and market trends.

❖ **Geographic Diversification:** Expand geographic footprint by investing in properties located in diverse geographic regions (urban centers, suburban markets, emerging markets) characterized by varying economic growth prospects, demographic trends, and regional market conditions influencing property values, rental demand, and investment performance. Diversify across regional markets to mitigate local market risks, leverage growth opportunities, and capture market cycles impacting real estate investments across different geographical locations supporting portfolio diversification benefits and strategic asset allocation strategies.

- ❖ **Market Research and Due Diligence:** Conduct thorough market research, demographic analysis, and economic forecasts to assess property market fundamentals, supply-demand dynamics, and competitive landscape influencing investment decisions across diversified property types and locations. Evaluate market conditions, regulatory environments, and investment opportunities aligned with portfolio diversification objectives, risk-adjusted return expectations, and long-term growth strategies facilitating informed investment decisions, portfolio optimization, and strategic asset allocation strategies promoting investment diversification and sustainable portfolio growth.

By integrating long-term growth strategies, portfolio diversification principles, and strategic investment planning, real estate investors can build resilient portfolios, capitalize on market opportunities, and achieve sustainable investment performance through diversified property holdings, sector allocation strategies, and geographic expansion strategies supporting financial goals, risk management objectives, and long-term wealth accumulation in the dynamic real estate investment landscape.

Conclusion: Reflecting on Your Real Estate Journey

As you conclude your real estate journey or embark on the next phase of your investment strategy, reflecting on past experiences and adapting to evolving market changes and trends are critical for sustained success and growth in real estate investing. Throughout your journey, you've navigated through various stages, from initial property acquisitions to portfolio diversification and strategic growth initiatives. Each step has contributed to your knowledge, experience, and resilience in the dynamic real estate market landscape.

Reflecting on your real estate journey involves assessing achievements, challenges, and lessons learned to refine investment strategies, optimize portfolio performance, and align future goals with evolving market dynamics:

❖ **Achievements and Milestones:** Celebrate successes, property acquisitions, portfolio expansions, and financial milestones achieved through strategic planning, disciplined investment decisions, and proactive management strategies contributing to portfolio growth and investment profitability.

❖ **Challenges and Lessons Learned:** Acknowledge challenges, setbacks, or market uncertainties encountered throughout your real estate journey, emphasizing resilience, adaptive strategies, and problem-solving skills developed to overcome obstacles, mitigate risks, and navigate market volatility.

❖ **Skill Development and Growth:** Evaluate personal and professional growth, skill development in property management, financial analysis, risk assessment, and market research capabilities enhancing decision-making processes, operational efficiencies, and investment outcomes supporting long-term portfolio sustainability and investor success.

❖ **Portfolio Performance Review:** Conduct portfolio performance reviews, analyze investment returns, cash flow projections, and asset valuation metrics to assess portfolio health, identify underperforming assets or growth opportunities, and implement corrective actions or strategic adjustments aligned with investment objectives, risk tolerance, and market conditions influencing real estate investment decisions.

Adapting to Market Changes and Trends

Adapting to market changes and trends requires proactive monitoring, strategic planning, and responsiveness to evolving economic, regulatory, and consumer trends shaping real estate investment opportunities and portfolio management strategies:

- ❖ **Market Analysis and Forecasting:** Stay informed on market trends, economic indicators, and demographic shifts impacting real estate markets, property values, rental demand, and investment returns. Conduct market research, leverage industry insights, and engage with real estate professionals to anticipate market changes, identify emerging opportunities, and adjust investment strategies to capitalize on evolving market dynamics.

- ❖ **Technology Integration:** Embrace technological advancements, data analytics, and digital platforms enhancing property management efficiency, tenant engagement, and operational transparency. Adopt property management software, online marketing tools, and smart building technologies to streamline operations, optimize resource allocation, and leverage data-driven insights for informed decision-making supporting portfolio growth and performance optimization.

❖ **Sustainability and ESG Initiatives:** Incorporate environmental, social, and governance (ESG) principles into investment strategies, promoting sustainable development practices, energy-efficient property upgrades, and community engagement initiatives enhancing property value, tenant satisfaction, and regulatory compliance in alignment with corporate responsibility goals and investor preferences.

❖ **Risk Management Strategies:** Implement risk management strategies, including portfolio diversification, asset allocation adjustments, and contingency planning for economic downturns, market volatility, or unforeseen events impacting real estate investments. Hedge against financial risks, interest rate fluctuations, and tenant turnover risks through lease diversification, insurance coverage, and capital reserves supporting portfolio resilience and long-term investment sustainability.

Reflecting on your real estate journey and adapting to market changes and trends are essential for navigating the dynamic real estate landscape, achieving investment success, and sustaining portfolio growth over the long term. Embrace continuous learning, innovation, and strategic planning to capitalize on market opportunities, mitigate risks, and optimize investment returns while aligning with evolving investor priorities, market demands, and regulatory requirements shaping the future of real estate investing.

By leveraging past experiences, embracing adaptive strategies, and remaining resilient amidst market challenges, you position yourself to thrive in the competitive real estate industry, achieve financial objectives, and build a legacy of successful real estate investments contributing to personal wealth accumulation, portfolio diversification, and long-term prosperity in the global marketplace.

www.ingramcontent.com/pod-product-compliance
Lightning Source LLC
Chambersburg PA
CBHW071932210526
45479CB00002B/651